The Affiliate Marketing Cheat Sheet: A Step-by-Step Guide to Maximizing Your Earnings

Roy Hendershot

Published by Roy Hendershot, 2024.

While every precaution has been taken in the preparation of this book, the publisher assumes no responsibility for errors or omissions, or for damages resulting from the use of the information contained herein.

THE AFFILIATE MARKETING CHEAT SHEET: A STEP-BY-STEP GUIDE TO MAXIMIZING YOUR EARNINGS

First edition. June 15, 2024.

Written by Roy Hendershot.

Table of Contents

Chapter 1: Understanding Affiliate Marketing

———

Affiliate marketing is like being a middleman in a sales transaction, but instead of selling products yourself, you promote them and earn a commission on every sale made through your referral. Imagine you're telling your friends about a fantastic new toy you found. If they buy it because of your recommendation, you get a small piece of the sale. That's the essence of affiliate marketing, and it's a powerful way to make money online without having to create your own products.

The history of affiliate marketing dates back to the mid-1990s. It started with a little company called Amazon, which needed a way to boost sales. They decided to pay people a commission for referring customers to their website. This idea caught on like wildfire, and soon, other companies were offering similar programs. Today, affiliate marketing is a multi-billion dollar industry with opportunities for anyone willing to put in the effort.

Affiliate marketing works by connecting three parties: the merchant, the affiliate, and the customer. The merchant is the one who owns the product or service. The affiliate is the person who promotes the product, and the customer is the one who buys it. When the customer makes a purchase, the merchant pays a commission to the affiliate for bringing in the sale. This win-win-win scenario has made affiliate marketing a popular choice for online entrepreneurs.

To succeed in affiliate marketing, you need to understand some key terms and concepts. For example, a cookie is a small piece of data stored on a customer's computer that tracks their activity. When a customer clicks on your affiliate link, a cookie is placed on their device. This allows the merchant to know that you referred the customer and ensures you get credit for the sale, even if the purchase is made days or weeks later.

Affiliates come in all shapes and sizes, from individuals running small blogs to large companies with extensive marketing teams. What they all have in common is the goal of driving traffic to the merchant's site and earning commissions. Some affiliates focus on a single niche, while others promote a wide range of products. The flexibility of affiliate marketing allows you to choose what works best for you and your audience.

Merchants also vary widely. Some are small businesses with a single product, while others are large corporations with thousands of items. What they all need are affiliates to help them reach more customers. By partnering with affiliates, merchants can expand their marketing reach without spending a fortune on advertising. This makes affiliate marketing an attractive option for businesses of all sizes.

Tracking is a crucial part of affiliate marketing. It allows merchants to monitor the performance of their affiliates and ensure they are getting paid for the sales they generate. This is typically done through affiliate networks, which provide tracking software and other tools to help manage the relationship between merchants and affiliates. Understanding how tracking works will help you optimize your efforts and maximize your earnings.

Commissions are the payments you receive for generating sales. These can be a fixed amount or a percentage of the sale. Some programs also offer performance bonuses or tiered commission structures that reward you for driving higher volumes of sales. Knowing the different types of commissions can help you choose the best programs for your needs.

There are several types of affiliate programs, including pay-per-sale, pay-per-click, and pay-per-lead. Pay-per-sale programs pay you a commission for each sale you generate. Pay-per-click programs pay you for each click on your affiliate links, regardless of whether a sale is made. Pay-per-lead programs pay you for generating leads, such as sign-ups or registrations. Understanding these models will help you choose the right programs to join.

The affiliate marketing ecosystem is made up of many different players, including merchants, affiliates, networks, and customers. Each plays a vital role in the process, and understanding how they interact will help you navigate the industry more effectively. Affiliate networks act as intermediaries between merchants and affiliates, providing tracking, reporting, and payment processing services.

One of the main benefits of affiliate marketing is that it allows you to make money online without having to create your own products. This means you can focus on promoting products you believe in and let the merchants handle the rest. Additionally, affiliate marketing offers flexibility and scalability, allowing you to work from anywhere and grow your business at your own pace.

Despite its many benefits, affiliate marketing also comes with challenges. It can be competitive, and success often requires a significant amount of time and effort. Additionally, staying compliant with laws and regulations is crucial to avoid penalties. However, with the right strategies and a willingness to learn, you can overcome these challenges and build a successful affiliate marketing business.

Choosing your path in affiliate marketing involves deciding whether you want to be an affiliate or a merchant. Both roles offer unique opportunities and challenges. As an affiliate, you can promote a variety of products and earn commissions without the responsibility of product creation. As a merchant, you can leverage affiliates to boost sales and reach new customers.

Ethical considerations are important in affiliate marketing. Being honest and transparent with your audience builds trust and credibility. This means disclosing your affiliate relationships and ensuring the products you promote are of high quality. Ethical marketing practices not only benefit your audience but also help you build a sustainable business.

Legal requirements vary by region, but common regulations include disclosing affiliate relationships and adhering to advertising standards. Familiarizing yourself with these laws will help you stay compliant and avoid potential legal issues. This includes understanding the guidelines set by the Federal Trade Commission (FTC) in the United States.

There are many myths about affiliate marketing, such as the idea that it's an easy way to get rich quick. In reality, success in affiliate marketing requires hard work, patience, and persistence. Debunking these myths can help you set realistic expectations and focus on building a solid foundation for your business.

Popular affiliate niches include health and wellness, technology, personal finance, and lifestyle. Choosing a niche that aligns with your interests and expertise can make the process more enjoyable and increase your chances of success. Researching popular niches will give you insights into what works and help you find opportunities to stand out.

Case studies of successful affiliates can provide valuable insights and inspiration. Learning from their experiences and strategies can help you avoid common mistakes and find new ways to grow your business. Look for case studies that are relevant to your niche and study them to see what you can apply to your own efforts.

There are many tools available to help you succeed in affiliate marketing, including keyword research tools, SEO software, and analytics platforms. Investing in the right tools can save you time and help you make data-driven decisions. Familiarizing yourself with these tools will give you a competitive edge.

Industry trends and predictions can help you stay ahead of the curve and adapt to changes in the market. Keeping an eye on emerging trends will allow you to capitalize on new opportunities and adjust your strategies accordingly. This includes staying informed about technological advancements and shifts in consumer behavior.

Joining affiliate networks can provide access to a wide range of programs and tools to help you succeed. These networks act as intermediaries between merchants and affiliates, offering tracking, reporting, and payment processing services. Choosing the right networks will give you access to high-quality programs and support.

Creating a business plan is essential for success in affiliate marketing. This plan should outline your goals, strategies, and the steps you will take to achieve them. A well-thought-out plan will help you stay focused and organized, ensuring you stay on track as you build your business.

Setting realistic goals is crucial for maintaining motivation and measuring progress. Start with achievable targets and gradually increase them as you gain experience and confidence. This approach will help you build momentum and keep you motivated to continue growing your business.

Preparing for the journey ahead involves understanding that success in affiliate marketing takes time and effort. Stay committed, be patient, and keep learning. With dedication and the right strategies, you can build a successful affiliate marketing business that provides long-term income and fulfillment.

As you move forward, remember that choosing the right niche is the next critical step in your affiliate marketing journey. Let's dive into how

6

to select a niche that aligns with your interests and has the potential for profitability.

Chapter 2: Choosing the Right Niche

———

Choosing the right niche is like picking the perfect playground for your affiliate marketing business. It's where you'll spend your time, and it's essential to select a niche that you're passionate about and that has the potential for profitability. A niche is a specific segment of the market that you focus on, such as health and wellness, technology, or personal finance. By narrowing your focus, you can become an expert in your chosen area and build a loyal audience.

The importance of niche selection cannot be overstated. A well-chosen niche can make the difference between success and failure in affiliate marketing. It helps you stand out in a crowded market and connect with a specific audience that is interested in what you have to offer. When you choose a niche that you're passionate about, it becomes easier to create engaging content and maintain your motivation over the long term.

Identifying your interests is the first step in choosing a niche. Think about the topics you enjoy and the activities you love. Your hobbies, skills, and experiences can provide valuable insights into potential niches. For example, if you love cooking, a food-related niche could be a great fit. If you're into fitness, consider a niche focused on exercise and nutrition.

Market research is crucial for finding a profitable niche. Start by exploring popular topics and trends within your areas of interest. Use online tools and resources to analyze market demand and competition. Google Trends, keyword research tools, and social media platforms can help you identify what people are searching for and talking about. Look for niches with a high level of interest but moderate competition.

Tools for niche research can make the process more efficient and effective. Keyword research tools like Ahrefs, SEMrush, and Google

Keyword Planner can help you find popular search terms related to your interests. Social media platforms like Facebook, Instagram, and Pinterest can provide insights into trending topics and audience engagement. Use these tools to gather data and make informed decisions about your niche.

Analyzing market demand involves looking at the popularity of topics within your chosen niche. Check search volumes for relevant keywords and assess the level of interest on social media. Look for niches with consistent or growing demand, as these are more likely to provide long-term opportunities. Avoid niches that are too narrow or have declining interest.

Assessing competition is another critical step. High competition can make it challenging to stand out, especially if you're just starting. Look at the top websites and influencers in your potential niches and evaluate their content, audience, and engagement. If the competition is too fierce, consider finding a unique angle or sub-niche that allows you to differentiate yourself.

Profitability factors include the potential for monetization and the availability of affiliate programs. Some niches, like technology and finance, tend to have higher commission rates and more opportunities for affiliate partnerships. Research the affiliate programs available in your niche and evaluate their commission structures, product quality, and support. Choosing a niche with strong monetization potential will help you maximize your earnings.

Audience analysis is essential for understanding who your potential customers are and what they need. Create a profile of your ideal audience, including their demographics, interests, and pain points. This will help you create targeted content and marketing strategies that resonate with your audience. Understanding your audience's needs and preferences will also guide your product recommendations and promotions.

Choosing a sustainable niche means selecting one with long-term potential. Avoid fads and trends that may lose popularity quickly. Instead, focus on evergreen topics that have consistent demand over time. This will help you build a stable and lasting business that can adapt to changes in the market.

Case studies of successful niches can provide valuable insights and inspiration. Look at examples of affiliates who have thrived in different niches and analyze their strategies. Pay attention to their content, marketing techniques, and audience engagement. Learning from their experiences can help you avoid common mistakes and find new opportunities.

Niche trends and opportunities are constantly evolving, and staying informed can give you a competitive edge. Follow industry news, subscribe to relevant blogs, and join online communities to keep up with the latest developments. This will help you identify emerging trends and adapt your strategies accordingly.

Balancing passion and profit is crucial for long-term success. While it's important to choose a niche you're passionate about, it's equally important to ensure it has the potential for profitability. Finding the right balance will make your work more enjoyable and sustainable. Don't be afraid to explore different niches until you find the perfect fit.

Avoiding oversaturated niches can be challenging, but it's essential for standing out. Look for niches with moderate competition and find unique angles or sub-niches that allow you to differentiate yourself. This could involve focusing on a specific audience segment, offering unique content, or providing valuable insights that others overlook.

Finding your unique angle is about identifying what sets you apart from others in your niche. This could be your personal experience, expertise, or a unique perspective. Highlighting your unique selling points will help you attract and retain a loyal audience. Think about what makes you different and how you can leverage that to your advantage.

Building authority in your niche involves establishing yourself as a trusted expert. This requires consistent, high-quality content that provides value to your audience. Engage with your audience through comments, social media, and email to build relationships and trust. Over time, your authority will grow, and you'll become a go-to resource in your niche.

Creating content for your niche is an ongoing process that requires creativity and dedication. Focus on providing value to your audience by addressing their needs and solving their problems. This could include blog posts, videos, podcasts, and social media updates. Consistency is key, so create a content schedule and stick to it.

Engaging your audience is crucial for building a loyal following. Respond to comments and messages, ask for feedback, and create interactive content that encourages participation. Building a community around your niche will help you retain your audience and increase your influence.

Expanding your niche over time involves exploring new topics and opportunities within your chosen area. This could include adding new content formats, collaborating with other influencers, or launching new products. Continuously evolving your niche will help you stay relevant and attract new audiences.

Testing your niche is an ongoing process that involves experimenting with different strategies and measuring their effectiveness. Use analytics tools to track your performance and make data-driven decisions. Adjust your strategies based on what works and what doesn't. This iterative approach will help you optimize your efforts and maximize your success.

Adjusting your strategy is necessary as you learn more about your niche and audience. Be flexible and open to change, and don't be afraid to pivot if something isn't working. Continuous improvement is key to long-term success.

Long-term niche sustainability is about building a business that can adapt to changes in the market and continue to thrive. Focus on creating valuable content, building strong relationships with your audience, and staying informed about industry trends. This will help you maintain a stable and successful business over time.

Finalizing your niche choice involves making a decision based on your research and analysis. Once you've chosen your niche, commit to it and start building your platform. Remember that success takes time and effort, so stay dedicated and keep learning.

As we move forward, it's time to explore how to find affiliate programs that align with your niche and offer the best opportunities for success.

Chapter 3: Finding Affiliate Programs

———

Finding the right affiliate programs is like discovering a treasure trove of opportunities for your niche. These programs are the lifeblood of your affiliate marketing business, as they provide the products and services you'll promote to earn commissions. The key is to find programs that align with your niche, offer competitive commissions, and provide strong support.

Affiliate programs come in various shapes and sizes, each with its unique benefits and challenges. Some programs are part of large affiliate networks, while others are run directly by individual merchants. Understanding the different types of programs will help you make informed decisions and choose the ones that best suit your needs.

Evaluating affiliate programs involves looking at several factors, including commission rates, cookie duration, payment methods, and support. Commission rates vary widely, with some programs offering a percentage of the sale and others providing a fixed amount. Higher commission rates are attractive, but they often come with higher competition. Balancing commission rates with other factors will help you choose the best programs.

Cookie duration refers to the length of time a cookie remains active on a customer's device after they click your affiliate link. Longer cookie durations increase the likelihood of earning a commission, as customers may take time to make a purchase. Look for programs with generous cookie durations to maximize your earning potential.

Payment methods are another important consideration. Some programs pay via PayPal, while others use bank transfers, checks, or other methods. Choose programs that offer convenient and reliable payment options.

Additionally, consider the payment threshold, which is the minimum amount you need to earn before receiving a payout. Lower thresholds mean you'll get paid more frequently.

Support and resources provided by affiliate programs can significantly impact your success. Look for programs that offer comprehensive training, marketing materials, and dedicated affiliate managers. These resources can help you promote products more effectively and address any issues that arise. Strong support can make a big difference, especially if you're new to affiliate marketing.

Finding programs in your niche involves researching and exploring various options. Start by searching for affiliate programs related to your niche using search engines, affiliate directories, and social media. Look for programs that align with your niche and offer products or services that your audience will find valuable. Joining multiple programs can help diversify your income streams and reduce risk.

Top affiliate networks, such as Amazon Associates, ShareASale, and Commission Junction, offer a wide range of programs across various niches. These networks provide tracking, reporting, and payment processing services, making it easier to manage your affiliate relationships. Joining reputable networks can give you access to high-quality programs and reliable support.

Direct affiliate programs are run by individual merchants and can offer unique opportunities. These programs often provide higher commission rates and more personalized support compared to network programs. Research companies in your niche and look for affiliate programs on their websites. Building direct relationships with merchants can lead to exclusive deals and better opportunities.

Case studies of top affiliate programs can provide valuable insights into what works and what doesn't. Look at examples of successful affiliates and analyze the programs they promote. Pay attention to their strategies, content, and marketing techniques. Learning from their experiences can help you avoid common mistakes and find new opportunities.

Commission structures vary widely between programs. Some offer flat-rate commissions, while others provide a percentage of the sale. Additionally, some programs have tiered commission structures that reward you for driving higher volumes of sales. Understanding these structures will help you choose the programs that best align with your goals.

Payment methods and schedules are essential factors to consider. Some programs pay monthly, while others offer weekly or bi-weekly payouts. Choose programs that provide timely and reliable payments. Additionally, consider the payment options available, such as PayPal, bank transfer, or check. Opt for programs that offer convenient payment methods for you.

Terms and conditions are critical to understanding before joining an affiliate program. These documents outline the rules and requirements for participation, including how commissions are earned, payment schedules, and compliance guidelines. Reading and understanding these terms will help you avoid potential issues and ensure you're meeting the program's requirements.

Affiliate tools and resources can significantly impact your success. Look for programs that offer a range of marketing materials, such as banners, product images, and email templates. These resources can help you promote products more effectively and save you time. Additionally, training materials and webinars can provide valuable insights and tips for success.

Program support and training are essential for helping you succeed. Look for programs that offer dedicated affiliate managers, support forums, and comprehensive training materials. Having access to knowledgeable support can help you address any issues and optimize your marketing efforts. Strong support can make a significant difference, especially if you're new to affiliate marketing.

Navigating affiliate dashboards can be overwhelming, especially if you're new to affiliate marketing. These dashboards provide access to important information, such as your earnings, traffic, and performance metrics. Familiarize yourself with the dashboard layout and features to make the most of the tools available. This will help you track your progress and make data-driven decisions.

Tracking and reporting are crucial for monitoring your performance and optimizing your efforts. Look for programs that offer detailed reports on clicks, conversions, and earnings. Use this data to identify what's working and what's not, and adjust your strategies accordingly. Effective tracking and reporting will help you maximize your earnings and improve your overall performance.

Understanding conversion rates is essential for evaluating the effectiveness of your marketing efforts. Conversion rates represent the percentage of clicks that result in a sale. Higher conversion rates indicate more effective marketing and better alignment with your audience's needs. Analyze your conversion rates and look for ways to improve them, such as optimizing your landing pages and call-to-actions.

Case studies of program success can provide valuable insights into what works and what doesn't. Look at examples of affiliates who have thrived with specific programs and analyze their strategies. Pay attention to their content, marketing techniques, and audience engagement. Learning from their experiences can help you avoid common mistakes and find new opportunities.

Avoiding scam programs is crucial for protecting your reputation and ensuring you get paid for your efforts. Be wary of programs that promise unrealistic earnings, have poor reviews, or lack transparency. Research programs thoroughly before joining and look for red flags, such as hidden fees or unclear terms. Choosing reputable programs will help you build a trustworthy and successful business.

Building relationships with merchants can lead to exclusive deals and better opportunities. Reach out to program managers and express your interest in promoting their products. Building a rapport with merchants can lead to higher commission rates, exclusive offers, and personalized support. These relationships can be mutually beneficial and help you succeed in affiliate marketing.

Program compliance involves adhering to the rules and guidelines set by the affiliate program. This includes following advertising standards, disclosing affiliate relationships, and avoiding prohibited practices. Staying compliant will help you avoid penalties and maintain a positive relationship with the program. Understanding and following the rules is essential for long-term success.

Leveraging exclusive offers can help you stand out and attract more customers. Many programs offer special deals, discounts, and promotions that you can use to entice your audience. Highlight these offers in your marketing materials and create a sense of urgency to encourage purchases. Exclusive offers can increase your conversions and boost your earnings.

Promoting high-ticket items can significantly increase your earnings. High-ticket items are products or services with higher price points, resulting in higher commissions. Look for programs that offer high-ticket products and focus on promoting them to your audience. Providing detailed reviews and valuable insights can help you convince potential buyers and increase your sales.

Choosing long-term programs is essential for building a stable and sustainable business. Look for programs with a proven track record and a strong reputation. Avoid programs that seem temporary or have frequent changes in terms and conditions. Long-term programs provide stability and reliable income, allowing you to focus on growing your business.

Diversifying your programs can help reduce risk and increase your earning potential. Don't rely on a single program or product for your income. Join multiple programs that align with your niche and promote a variety of products. This diversification will help you weather changes in the market and provide multiple income streams.

As we move forward, it's time to focus on building your platform, the foundation of your affiliate marketing business. A strong platform will help you reach your audience and promote your chosen affiliate programs effectively.

Chapter 4: Building Your Platform

———

Building your platform is like setting up your own virtual storefront where you can showcase the products and services you're promoting. This platform will be the foundation of your affiliate marketing business, and it's crucial to create a strong, engaging presence that attracts and retains your audience. Whether you choose to create a website, blog, or social media presence, your platform is where your affiliate marketing journey truly begins.

Creating a website is often the first step for many affiliates. A website provides a central hub for your content and promotions, giving you control over your brand and message. When creating your website, choose a domain name that reflects your niche and is easy to remember. Use a reliable web hosting service to ensure your site is fast and secure. A well-designed website can significantly impact your credibility and success.

Setting up a blog is another popular option for affiliate marketers. A blog allows you to share valuable content, build relationships with your audience, and drive traffic to your affiliate links. Choose a content management system like WordPress, which is user-friendly and offers a range of customization options. Consistent blogging can help you establish authority in your niche and attract a loyal readership.

Social media presence is essential for reaching a broader audience and driving traffic to your website or blog. Choose the social media platforms that are most popular with your target audience and create engaging profiles. Share a mix of promotional content, valuable insights, and personal stories to connect with your followers. Social media can be a powerful tool for building brand awareness and driving traffic to your affiliate offers.

Building an email list is one of the most effective ways to engage with your audience and promote your affiliate products. Offer a valuable incentive, such as a free ebook or exclusive content, to encourage visitors to subscribe to your newsletter. Use an email marketing service to manage your list and send regular updates. Personalized email campaigns can drive conversions and build long-term relationships with your subscribers.

Content management systems (CMS) are essential for creating and managing your website or blog. WordPress is the most popular CMS, offering a wide range of plugins and themes to customize your site. Other options include Joomla, Drupal, and Wix. Choose a CMS that fits your needs and technical skills. A well-organized CMS can streamline your content creation process and improve your site's performance.

Web hosting options vary in terms of price, features, and performance. Shared hosting is affordable and suitable for beginners, while VPS and dedicated hosting offer more resources and control. Consider your site's traffic and needs when choosing a hosting plan. Reliable web hosting ensures your site is always available and performs well, which is crucial for retaining visitors and driving sales.

Designing your website involves creating a user-friendly layout that reflects your brand and niche. Use a clean, responsive design that looks good on all devices. Choose colors, fonts, and images that align with your brand identity. A well-designed website enhances user experience and encourages visitors to explore your content and affiliate offers.

Essential website pages include a homepage, about page, contact page, and blog. Your homepage should provide an overview of your site and guide visitors to your key content. The about page tells your story and builds trust with your audience. The contact page makes it easy for visitors to reach you, and the blog is where you share valuable content and promote your affiliate products. Organize your site to make it easy for visitors to navigate and find what they're looking for.

SEO basics for your website are crucial for attracting organic traffic. Use keyword research to identify the terms your audience is searching for and incorporate them into your content. Optimize your site's meta tags, headers, and images to improve search engine visibility. Building backlinks from reputable sites can also boost your rankings. Effective SEO strategies can drive more traffic to your site and increase your earning potential.

Content planning and strategy involve creating a schedule for your blog posts, social media updates, and email campaigns. Plan your content around the interests and needs of your audience, and aim to provide value with every piece. Consistent, high-quality content builds trust and authority, helping you attract and retain a loyal audience.

Blogging for affiliate marketing involves creating informative and engaging posts that promote your affiliate products. Write product reviews, how-to guides, and comparison articles to provide value to your readers. Use a conversational tone and include personal anecdotes to make your content relatable. Blogging can drive traffic to your affiliate links and increase your conversions.

Social media strategies for affiliate marketing include sharing a mix of content types, such as blog posts, videos, and infographics. Engage with your followers by responding to comments and messages, and use hashtags to increase your reach. Run social media ads to promote your affiliate products and drive traffic to your site. Effective social media marketing can boost your brand awareness and sales.

Engaging with your audience is crucial for building relationships and trust. Respond to comments on your blog and social media, ask for feedback, and create interactive content, such as polls and quizzes. Building a community around your brand will help you retain your audience and increase your influence.

Case studies of successful platforms can provide valuable insights and inspiration. Look at examples of affiliates who have built strong platforms and analyze their strategies. Pay attention to their content, design, and engagement techniques. Learning from their experiences can help you build a more effective platform and avoid common mistakes.

Email marketing techniques involve creating personalized and targeted campaigns to promote your affiliate products. Segment your email list based on subscriber interests and behavior, and send relevant content and offers. Use catchy subject lines and compelling calls-to-action to increase open and click-through rates. Email marketing can drive conversions and build long-term relationships with your audience.

Using landing pages is an effective way to promote specific products and capture leads. Create dedicated landing pages for your top affiliate offers, with clear calls-to-action and persuasive content. Optimize your landing pages for conversions by testing different elements, such as headlines, images, and buttons. Well-designed landing pages can significantly increase your conversion rates.

A/B testing for optimization involves experimenting with different versions of your content, design, and calls-to-action to see what performs best. Use A/B testing tools to compare variations and make data-driven decisions. Continuous testing and optimization can help you improve your site's performance and increase your earnings.

Tools for managing your platform include content management systems, SEO tools, social media schedulers, and email marketing services.

Investing in the right tools can save you time and help you make data-driven decisions. Familiarizing yourself with these tools will give you a competitive edge and streamline your workflow.

Automation tools can help you save time and increase efficiency. Use tools like Zapier to automate repetitive tasks, such as posting to social media or sending email updates. Automation can free up your time to focus on creating valuable content and building relationships with your audience.

Integrating analytics into your platform is essential for tracking your performance and making informed decisions. Use tools like Google Analytics to monitor your traffic, conversions, and user behavior. Analyze your data regularly to identify trends and opportunities for improvement. Effective use of analytics can help you optimize your efforts and maximize your success.

Mobile optimization is crucial for reaching the growing number of users who access the internet on their mobile devices. Ensure your website is responsive and looks good on all screen sizes. Optimize your images and content for faster loading times, and use mobile-friendly design elements. Mobile optimization can improve user experience and increase your traffic and conversions.

Maintaining your platform involves regularly updating your content, monitoring your site's performance, and addressing any issues that arise. Keep your software and plugins up-to-date to ensure security and functionality. Regular maintenance will help you provide a better experience for your visitors and maintain your site's credibility.

As we move forward, it's time to focus on creating quality content that will attract and engage your audience. Quality content is the cornerstone of your affiliate marketing strategy and will help you build authority and drive sales.

Chapter 5: Creating Quality Content

Creating quality content is like cooking a delicious meal for your guests; it needs to be tasty, well-presented, and satisfying. In the world of affiliate marketing, your content is what draws people in, keeps them engaged, and encourages them to take action. High-quality content can build trust, establish you as an authority in your niche, and drive traffic to your affiliate links.

The importance of quality content cannot be overstated. Good content provides value to your audience, answers their questions, and solves their problems. It helps you build a loyal following and encourages people to return to your site. In affiliate marketing, quality content is what drives conversions and ultimately, your earnings. Without it, your efforts may fall flat.

There are many types of affiliate content, each serving a different purpose. Product reviews are one of the most common forms of affiliate content. They provide detailed information about a product, highlighting its features, benefits, and potential drawbacks. A well-written review can help potential buyers make an informed decision and encourage them to purchase through your affiliate link.

How-to guides are another valuable type of content. These guides provide step-by-step instructions on how to use a product or achieve a specific goal. They are educational and often solve a problem for your audience, making them highly engaging. How-to guides can attract traffic from search engines and drive conversions by showing the practical benefits of a product.

Comparison articles compare multiple products or services, highlighting their pros and cons. These articles help your audience make informed choices by presenting different options side by side. Comparison articles can be particularly effective in niches with many competing products, as they provide a comprehensive overview and guide readers toward the best choice.

Listicles are popular because they are easy to read and share. These articles present information in a list format, such as "Top 10 Tips for Healthy Eating" or "5 Best Gadgets for Home Office." Listicles can cover a wide range of topics and are great for attracting traffic and engaging readers. They also provide opportunities to include multiple affiliate links within a single article.

Case studies showcase real-life examples of how a product or service has helped someone achieve a goal. These stories provide proof of the product's effectiveness and can be highly persuasive. Case studies are particularly powerful because they combine storytelling with factual information, making them both engaging and convincing.

Videos and podcasts are increasingly popular forms of content. Videos allow you to demonstrate products, share tutorials, and engage with your audience visually. Podcasts provide an opportunity to share insights, interviews, and discussions in an audio format. Both formats can help you reach a wider audience and create a more personal connection with your followers.

Infographics are visual representations of information that make complex topics easier to understand. They are highly shareable and can drive traffic to your site from social media and other platforms. Infographics can complement your written content and provide additional value to your audience.

Webinars are live or recorded online presentations that allow you to engage with your audience in real time. They are excellent for providing in-depth information, answering questions, and promoting products.

Webinars can build trust and credibility, making them an effective tool for driving conversions.

Ebooks and reports are long-form content that provide detailed information on a specific topic. They can be used as lead magnets to grow your email list or as paid products to generate revenue. Ebooks and reports allow you to showcase your expertise and provide significant value to your audience.

Content planning is essential for maintaining consistency and quality. Create a content calendar to plan your blog posts, social media updates, and email campaigns. This will help you stay organized and ensure you are regularly publishing new content. Planning also allows you to align your content with important dates and events in your niche.

Writing compelling headlines is crucial for attracting readers. A good headline should be clear, engaging, and relevant to the content. It should grab the reader's attention and make them want to learn more. Experiment with different headline styles and use tools like CoSchedule's Headline Analyzer to optimize your headlines for maximum impact.

Structuring your content involves organizing it in a way that is easy to read and understand. Use headings, subheadings, and bullet points to break up large blocks of text. Include images, videos, and other multimedia elements to enhance the content. A well-structured article improves readability and keeps your audience engaged.

SEO for content involves optimizing your articles to rank higher in search engine results. Use keyword research to identify the terms your audience is searching for and incorporate them into your content naturally. Optimize your meta tags, headers, and images to improve search engine visibility. Building backlinks from reputable sites can also boost your rankings.

Using keywords effectively is crucial for attracting organic traffic. Include your primary keywords in the title, headers, and throughout the content. Avoid keyword stuffing, which can harm your rankings. Focus on providing valuable information that naturally incorporates relevant keywords. This will help you attract more visitors and improve your search engine rankings.

Engaging your audience involves creating content that resonates with them. Use a conversational tone, share personal anecdotes, and ask questions to encourage interaction. Respond to comments and messages to build a sense of community. Engaging content keeps readers coming back and increases the likelihood of conversions.

Case studies of effective content can provide inspiration and insights. Look at examples of high-performing articles, videos, and other content in your niche. Analyze what makes them successful, such as their structure, style, and promotion strategies. Learning from successful content creators can help you improve your own efforts.

Content promotion strategies are essential for reaching a wider audience. Share your content on social media, email newsletters, and other platforms. Collaborate with influencers and other content creators to expand your reach. Use paid advertising to promote your top-performing content. Effective promotion can drive more traffic to your site and increase your earnings.

Social media content involves creating posts, images, videos, and other media to share on platforms like Facebook, Instagram, and Twitter. Tailor your content to each platform's audience and format. Engage with your followers by responding to comments and messages. Social media content can drive traffic to your site and increase your brand awareness.

Email content involves creating newsletters, updates, and promotional messages for your subscribers. Personalize your emails to make them more relevant and engaging. Include links to your latest content and affiliate offers. Email marketing can drive conversions and build long-term relationships with your audience.

Updating old content is an effective way to improve its performance. Refresh outdated information, add new insights, and optimize for current SEO trends. Republish updated content to give it a new lease on life. Regularly updating your content ensures it remains valuable and relevant to your audience.

Repurposing content involves turning your existing content into different formats. For example, you can turn a blog post into a video, infographic, or podcast episode. Repurposing allows you to reach new audiences and get more mileage out of your content. It also saves time and resources by leveraging your existing work.

Measuring content success involves tracking key metrics like traffic, engagement, and conversions. Use analytics tools to monitor your performance and identify areas for improvement. Experiment with different strategies and optimize your content based on the data. Regular analysis helps you make informed decisions and improve your results.

As we move forward, it's time to focus on driving traffic to your site, which is essential for reaching a larger audience and increasing your conversions.

Chapter 6: Driving Traffic to Your Site

———

Driving traffic to your site is like inviting people to a party; you need to make it enticing enough for them to show up and stay. In affiliate marketing, traffic is the lifeblood of your business. The more people who visit your site, the higher the chances of them clicking on your affiliate links and making purchases. Effective traffic generation strategies can significantly impact your success and earnings.

The importance of traffic cannot be overstated. Without visitors, your content goes unnoticed, and your affiliate links remain unclicked. Driving traffic to your site involves attracting and engaging your target audience, encouraging them to explore your content, and ultimately, converting them into customers. A steady stream of traffic is essential for maintaining and growing your affiliate marketing business.

Organic traffic strategies involve attracting visitors through search engines, social media, and other free channels. These strategies focus on creating valuable content that ranks well in search engine results and engages your audience. Organic traffic is often more sustainable and cost-effective than paid traffic, making it a crucial part of your overall strategy.

SEO for traffic is one of the most effective organic strategies. Optimizing your content for search engines involves using relevant keywords, creating high-quality content, and building backlinks from reputable sites. Focus on providing valuable information that answers your audience's questions and solves their problems. Effective SEO can drive a significant amount of traffic to your site over time.

Creating shareable content is another key strategy. When your content resonates with your audience, they are more likely to share it with their friends and followers. This increases your reach and drives more traffic to your site. Focus on creating engaging, informative, and entertaining content that people will want to share. Use eye-catching images, compelling headlines, and interactive elements to enhance your content's shareability.

Social media traffic involves using platforms like Facebook, Instagram, Twitter, and LinkedIn to drive visitors to your site. Share your content regularly, engage with your followers, and use hashtags to increase your visibility. Participate in relevant groups and communities to connect with potential readers. Social media can be a powerful tool for driving traffic and building brand awareness.

Leveraging social media ads can boost your reach and drive targeted traffic to your site. Platforms like Facebook and Instagram offer detailed targeting options, allowing you to reach specific demographics and interests. Create compelling ad copy and visuals to attract attention and encourage clicks. Social media ads can be a cost-effective way to drive traffic and increase your conversions.

Using influencers can amplify your reach and drive more traffic to your site. Partner with influencers in your niche who have a large and engaged following. Collaborate on content, such as guest posts, product reviews, and social media shoutouts. Influencer marketing can help you tap into new audiences and build credibility with potential customers.

Guest blogging is an effective way to reach new audiences and drive traffic to your site. Write high-quality articles for reputable blogs in your niche and include links back to your site. Guest blogging can increase your visibility, establish you as an authority, and drive referral traffic. Choose blogs with a large and engaged readership for the best results.

Forum participation involves engaging with online communities related to your niche. Join forums, such as Reddit, Quora, and niche-specific boards, and contribute valuable insights and answers. Include links to your content where relevant, but avoid being overly promotional. Participating in forums can drive targeted traffic and build your reputation as an expert.

Paid traffic strategies involve using advertising platforms to drive visitors to your site. Google Ads, Facebook Ads, and other platforms allow you to create targeted campaigns that reach specific audiences. Paid traffic can provide quick results and help you scale your efforts. However, it requires a budget and careful management to ensure a positive return on investment.

Google Ads is one of the most popular paid traffic platforms. It allows you to create search, display, and video ads that appear on Google and its partner sites. Use keyword research to target relevant search terms and create compelling ad copy to attract clicks. Monitor your campaigns closely and optimize them for the best performance.

Facebook Ads offers detailed targeting options and a range of ad formats, including image, video, carousel, and slideshow ads. Use Facebook's targeting features to reach specific demographics, interests, and behaviors. Create engaging ad copy and visuals to capture attention and drive traffic to your site. Facebook Ads can be highly effective for reaching a large and diverse audience.

Other ad platforms, such as Instagram, Twitter, LinkedIn, and Pinterest, offer unique opportunities for driving traffic. Each platform has its strengths and best practices, so tailor your campaigns to fit the platform and your target audience. Experiment with different ad formats and strategies to find what works best for you.

Retargeting campaigns involve targeting visitors who have previously visited your site but did not convert. Use retargeting ads to remind them of your content and encourage them to return. Retargeting can be highly effective for increasing conversions, as it targets people who are already familiar with your brand. Use platforms like Google Ads and Facebook Ads for retargeting campaigns.

Email marketing for traffic involves using your email list to drive visitors to your site. Send regular newsletters with links to your latest content, promotions, and affiliate offers. Segment your list to send targeted messages based on subscriber interests and behavior. Email marketing can drive significant traffic and build long-term relationships with your audience.

Building backlinks from reputable sites can boost your search engine rankings and drive referral traffic. Reach out to bloggers, journalists, and influencers in your niche and offer to collaborate on content. Create valuable resources, such as infographics and ebooks, that others will want to link to. High-quality backlinks can improve your site's authority and visibility.

Collaborations and partnerships with other content creators can expand your reach and drive traffic to your site. Co-create content, such as webinars, podcasts, and guest posts, to share with each other's audiences. Collaborations can introduce you to new audiences and provide mutual benefits. Look for partners who share your target audience and values.

Offline traffic strategies involve promoting your site through traditional marketing methods, such as print advertising, business cards, and events. Include your website URL on all marketing materials and encourage people to visit your site. Attend industry conferences, trade shows, and networking events to connect with potential readers. Offline strategies can complement your online efforts and drive additional traffic.

Mobile traffic is increasingly important as more people access the internet on their smartphones and tablets. Ensure your website is mobile-friendly and provides a seamless experience on all devices.

Optimize your content for mobile users by using responsive design, fast loading times, and easy navigation. Mobile optimization can improve user experience and increase your traffic and conversions.

Traffic analysis tools, such as Google Analytics, provide valuable insights into your site's performance. Use these tools to monitor your traffic sources, user behavior, and conversion rates. Analyze your data to identify trends and opportunities for improvement. Regular analysis helps you make informed decisions and optimize your traffic generation strategies.

Adjusting traffic strategies involves experimenting with different approaches and optimizing your efforts based on the results. Test various content types, promotion methods, and advertising platforms to see what works best for your audience. Be flexible and open to change, and continuously refine your strategies for maximum effectiveness.

Long-term traffic growth requires consistent effort and adaptation. Focus on creating valuable content, building strong relationships with your audience, and staying informed about industry trends. Invest in both organic and paid traffic strategies to ensure a steady flow of visitors. Long-term growth will help you build a sustainable affiliate marketing business.

Traffic and conversion go hand in hand. Driving traffic to your site is only half the battle; you also need to convert those visitors into customers. As we move forward, we'll focus on converting traffic into sales, which is essential for maximizing your earnings and achieving your affiliate marketing goals.

Chapter 7: Converting Traffic into Sales

———

Converting traffic into sales is like turning a casual shopper into a paying customer. It's the crucial step where all your efforts in driving traffic pay off. Without conversions, your traffic is just numbers without value. Effective conversion strategies can significantly impact your earnings and ensure that your affiliate marketing efforts are worthwhile.

The importance of conversion cannot be overstated. While driving traffic to your site is essential, converting that traffic into sales is what ultimately generates revenue. Conversion involves guiding your visitors through the buyer's journey and encouraging them to take action, such as making a purchase or signing up for a service. High conversion rates mean more sales and higher earnings from your affiliate marketing efforts.

Understanding the buyer's journey is crucial for effective conversion. The buyer's journey consists of three main stages: awareness, consideration, and decision. In the awareness stage, potential customers become aware of a problem or need. In the consideration stage, they explore different solutions and evaluate their options. In the decision stage, they choose a product or service and make a purchase. Tailoring your content and strategies to each stage of the journey can help you convert more visitors into customers.

Optimizing landing pages is one of the most effective ways to increase conversions. A landing page is a dedicated page on your site designed to promote a specific product or offer. It should have a clear and compelling headline, engaging content, and a strong call-to-action. Use visuals, testimonials, and benefits to persuade visitors to take action. A well-optimized landing page can significantly boost your conversion rates.

Effective call-to-actions (CTAs) are essential for guiding visitors toward the desired action. CTAs should be clear, concise, and compelling. Use action-oriented language, such as "Buy Now," "Sign Up," or "Learn More." Place CTAs strategically throughout your content and make them stand out with contrasting colors and buttons. Effective CTAs can increase the likelihood of conversions and drive more sales.

Building trust with your audience is crucial for successful conversions. Trust is built through transparency, consistency, and value. Be honest about your affiliate relationships and provide accurate information about the products you promote. Consistently deliver high-quality content that addresses your audience's needs and solves their problems. Building trust encourages visitors to take action and become loyal customers.

Product page optimization involves creating detailed and persuasive product descriptions. Highlight the features, benefits, and unique selling points of the product. Use high-quality images and videos to showcase the product in action. Include customer reviews and testimonials to build credibility. Optimizing your product pages can help you persuade visitors to make a purchase and increase your conversion rates.

Using testimonials and reviews is an effective way to build trust and encourage conversions. Positive reviews and testimonials from satisfied customers provide social proof and reassure potential buyers. Include testimonials on your landing pages, product pages, and throughout your content. Encourage your audience to leave reviews and share their experiences with the products you promote.

Offering incentives can motivate visitors to take action. Incentives can include discounts, free trials, bonuses, or limited-time offers. Create a sense of urgency by highlighting the scarcity or time-sensitive nature of the offer. Incentives can increase the perceived value of the product and encourage visitors to make a purchase.

Creating urgency is a powerful conversion technique. Highlight limited-time offers, low stock levels, or exclusive deals to create a sense of urgency. Use countdown timers, limited availability messages, and special promotions to encourage visitors to act quickly. Urgency can drive immediate action and increase your conversion rates.

Email marketing for conversions involves using personalized and targeted email campaigns to promote your affiliate products. Segment your email list based on subscriber interests and behavior, and send relevant offers and content. Use compelling subject lines, engaging copy, and strong CTAs to encourage clicks and conversions. Email marketing can drive significant sales and build long-term relationships with your audience.

Segmentation and personalization are key strategies for effective email marketing. Segment your list based on demographics, behavior, and interests to send targeted messages. Personalize your emails with the recipient's name, relevant content, and tailored offers. Segmentation and personalization can increase open rates, click-through rates, and conversions.

A/B testing for conversion involves experimenting with different elements of your content, design, and CTAs to see what performs best. Test variations of headlines, images, copy, and buttons to identify the most effective combinations. Use A/B testing tools to compare results and make data-driven decisions. Continuous testing and optimization can help you improve your conversion rates over time.

Conversion rate optimization (CRO) involves analyzing and improving your site's performance to increase conversions. Use analytics tools to monitor user behavior, identify bottlenecks, and track conversion rates. Experiment with different strategies, such as optimizing your landing pages, refining your CTAs, and enhancing your content. Effective CRO can help you maximize your earnings and achieve your affiliate marketing goals.

Analyzing conversion data is essential for making informed decisions. Use tools like Google Analytics to track key metrics, such as bounce rates, click-through rates, and conversion rates. Analyze your data to identify trends, patterns, and areas for improvement. Data-driven decisions can help you optimize your strategies and increase your conversions.

Improving site speed can have a significant impact on conversions. Slow-loading pages can frustrate visitors and lead to higher bounce rates. Optimize your site's performance by compressing images, using a content delivery network (CDN), and minimizing code. A fast-loading site provides a better user experience and can increase your conversion rates.

Reducing cart abandonment is crucial for recovering lost sales. Cart abandonment occurs when visitors add items to their cart but leave without completing the purchase. Use strategies like sending cart abandonment emails, offering incentives, and simplifying the checkout process to reduce abandonment rates. Recovering abandoned carts can boost your sales and increase your earnings.

Handling objections involves addressing potential concerns or hesitations that visitors may have. Common objections include price, quality, and trust. Provide clear and convincing information to address these concerns, such as product guarantees, customer reviews, and detailed descriptions. Handling objections effectively can persuade visitors to make a purchase and increase your conversion rates.

Upselling and cross-selling are techniques to increase the value of each sale. Upselling involves encouraging customers to purchase a higher-priced or upgraded version of a product. Cross-selling involves recommending related products that complement the original purchase.

Use these techniques to maximize your revenue and provide additional value to your customers.

Building customer loyalty is essential for long-term success. Loyal customers are more likely to make repeat purchases and refer others to your site. Provide exceptional value, personalized experiences, and excellent customer service to build loyalty. Engage with your audience through email, social media, and other channels to foster strong relationships.

Using live chat can enhance the user experience and increase conversions. Live chat allows visitors to ask questions and receive immediate assistance. It can help address concerns, provide product information, and guide visitors through the buying process. Implementing live chat can improve customer satisfaction and boost your conversion rates.

Mobile conversion strategies involve optimizing your site for mobile users. Ensure your site is responsive and provides a seamless experience on all devices. Use mobile-friendly design elements, such as large buttons and simple navigation. Optimize your content for mobile readers by using short paragraphs, clear headings, and concise copy. Mobile optimization can improve user experience and increase your conversions.

Leveraging analytics involves using data to monitor your performance and make informed decisions. Use tools like Google Analytics to track key metrics, such as traffic, conversions, and user behavior. Analyze your data regularly to identify trends and opportunities for improvement. Data-driven decisions can help you optimize your strategies and increase your earnings.

As we move forward, it's time to focus on analyzing and optimizing your performance to ensure continuous improvement and long-term success in your affiliate marketing business.

Chapter 8: Analyzing and Optimizing Performance

Analyzing and optimizing performance is like fine-tuning a musical instrument; it ensures that everything works in harmony and produces the best possible results. In affiliate marketing, continuous analysis and optimization are essential for maximizing your earnings and achieving long-term success. By monitoring your performance and making data-driven decisions, you can improve your strategies and drive better results.

The importance of analysis cannot be overstated. Regularly monitoring your performance helps you understand what's working and what's not. It allows you to identify trends, patterns, and areas for improvement. Without analysis, you're essentially flying blind and missing opportunities to optimize your efforts. Effective analysis provides the insights needed to make informed decisions and achieve your goals.

Key metrics to track include traffic, conversions, click-through rates, and earnings. These metrics provide a comprehensive view of your performance and help you measure your success. Use tools like Google Analytics to monitor your traffic and identify where your visitors are coming from. Track your conversions to see how many visitors are taking the desired action, such as making a purchase or signing up for a newsletter.

Using Google Analytics is essential for gaining insights into your site's performance. This powerful tool allows you to track key metrics, such as page views, bounce rates, and session duration. It also provides valuable data on user behavior, such as the most visited pages and the paths users take through your site. Analyzing this data helps you understand your audience and optimize your content and strategies.

Traffic analysis involves monitoring the sources of your traffic and identifying which channels are driving the most visitors. This includes organic search, social media, email, and referral traffic. Understanding your traffic sources helps you allocate your resources effectively and focus on the channels that provide the best results. Use this data to refine your marketing strategies and drive more targeted traffic to your site.

Conversion analysis is crucial for understanding how well your site is converting visitors into customers. Track key conversion metrics, such as conversion rates, average order value, and revenue per visitor. Analyze your conversion data to identify trends and patterns, such as which pages and products are performing best. Use this information to optimize your conversion strategies and increase your earnings.

Sales funnel analysis involves monitoring the different stages of the buyer's journey and identifying areas where visitors drop off. This includes analyzing metrics like funnel conversion rates, cart abandonment rates, and checkout completion rates. Use this data to identify bottlenecks and optimize your sales funnel to guide visitors smoothly through the buying process.

Case studies of performance analysis can provide valuable insights and inspiration. Look at examples of successful affiliates who have used data-driven strategies to optimize their performance. Analyze their techniques, such as A/B testing, user behavior analysis, and traffic segmentation. Learning from their experiences can help you apply similar strategies to your own efforts.

A/B testing strategies involve experimenting with different variations of your content, design, and CTAs to see what performs best. Use A/B testing tools to compare variations and measure their impact on key metrics. Test elements like headlines, images, copy, and buttons to identify the most effective combinations. Continuous testing and optimization can help you improve your performance over time.

Optimizing campaigns involves refining your marketing strategies based on data analysis. Use your performance data to identify underperforming areas and make adjustments. This could include optimizing your ad targeting, refining your content, or improving your CTAs. Regularly reviewing and optimizing your campaigns ensures you get the best possible results.

Analyzing content performance is essential for understanding what resonates with your audience. Track metrics like page views, time on page, and social shares to gauge the effectiveness of your content. Identify high-performing content and replicate its success by creating similar pieces. Analyzing your content performance helps you create more engaging and valuable content for your audience.

Adjusting SEO strategies involves optimizing your site and content based on search engine performance data. Use tools like Google Search Console to monitor your search rankings, click-through rates, and keyword performance. Identify opportunities to improve your SEO, such as updating old content, optimizing meta tags, and building backlinks. Effective SEO strategies can drive more organic traffic to your site.

Social media performance analysis involves tracking metrics like engagement rates, follower growth, and referral traffic. Use social media analytics tools to monitor your performance on platforms like Facebook, Instagram, and Twitter. Analyze your data to identify which types of content and posting times generate the most engagement. Optimize your social media strategies to increase your reach and drive more traffic.

Email marketing analysis involves tracking key metrics like open rates, click-through rates, and conversion rates. Use email marketing tools to monitor your campaign performance and identify areas for improvement. Segment your email list and analyze the performance of different segments to create more targeted and effective campaigns. Email marketing analysis helps you optimize your efforts and increase your conversions.

Using heatmaps provides insights into how visitors interact with your site. Heatmaps visually represent where users click, scroll, and spend the most time. Use heatmap tools to identify areas of high and low engagement on your pages. Optimize your design and content based on this data to improve user experience and increase conversions.

User behavior analysis involves tracking how visitors navigate your site and interact with your content. Use tools like session recordings and user flow reports to gain insights into user behavior. Identify common paths and drop-off points to optimize your site structure and content. Understanding user behavior helps you create a more intuitive and engaging experience.

Competitor analysis involves monitoring the performance of other affiliates in your niche. Identify your top competitors and analyze their strategies, content, and performance. Use tools like SEMrush and Ahrefs to track their traffic, backlinks, and keyword rankings. Learning from your competitors can provide valuable insights and help you identify opportunities for improvement.

Case studies of optimization success can provide inspiration and practical tips. Look at examples of affiliates who have successfully optimized their performance and achieved significant results. Analyze their strategies, such as A/B testing, CRO techniques, and data-driven decision-making. Learning from their success can help you apply similar techniques to your own efforts.

Reporting and dashboards provide a comprehensive view of your performance metrics. Use reporting tools to create custom dashboards that track your key metrics in real-time. Regularly review your reports to monitor your progress and identify trends. Dashboards provide a visual representation of your data, making it easier to analyze and make informed decisions.

Making data-driven decisions involves using your performance data to guide your strategies and actions. Analyze your data regularly to identify areas for improvement and opportunities for growth. Use data insights to optimize your content, marketing campaigns, and overall strategy. Data-driven decisions help you maximize your performance and achieve your goals.

Long-term optimization requires a commitment to continuous improvement. Regularly review your performance data, test new strategies, and make adjustments based on your findings. Stay informed about industry trends and best practices to ensure you're always optimizing effectively. Long-term optimization helps you build a sustainable and successful affiliate marketing business.

Tools for analysis include Google Analytics, Google Search Console, SEMrush, Ahrefs, and various A/B testing and heatmap tools. Invest in the right tools to gain comprehensive insights into your performance. Familiarize yourself with these tools and use them regularly to monitor your progress and optimize your efforts.

Setting new goals is essential for maintaining motivation and measuring success. Use your performance data to set realistic and achievable goals. Regularly review and adjust your goals based on your progress and changes in the market. Setting and achieving goals helps you stay focused and continuously improve your performance.

Continuous improvement is key to long-term success in affiliate marketing. Regularly analyze your performance, test new strategies, and optimize your efforts. Stay committed to learning and adapting to changes in the market. Continuous improvement helps you stay competitive and achieve your goals.

Avoiding analysis paralysis involves balancing data analysis with action. While it's important to analyze your performance, don't get bogged down in the details. Use your data to make informed decisions, but also take action and implement changes. Avoiding analysis paralysis helps you maintain momentum and achieve results.

As we move forward, it's time to focus on scaling your affiliate marketing business to reach new heights and achieve even greater success.

Chapter 9: Scaling Your Affiliate Marketing Business

―――

Scaling your affiliate marketing business is like adding more fuel to a well-oiled machine; it powers you to reach new heights and achieve greater success. Once you've established a solid foundation and optimized your performance, it's time to focus on growth and expansion. Scaling involves increasing your efforts, exploring new opportunities, and maximizing your earning potential.

Introduction to scaling involves understanding that growth is a continuous process. Scaling doesn't happen overnight; it requires careful planning, dedication, and a willingness to adapt. The goal is to build on your existing success and expand your reach, audience, and revenue streams. By scaling effectively, you can achieve sustainable growth and long-term success.

Outsourcing basics involve delegating tasks to others to free up your time and focus on high-impact activities. Outsourcing can include hiring freelancers for content creation, graphic design, social media management, and more. Use platforms like Upwork, Fiverr, and Freelancer to find skilled professionals. Outsourcing allows you to leverage the expertise of others and scale your efforts more efficiently.

Hiring freelancers involves finding and vetting the right candidates for your needs. Clearly define the tasks and skills required, and create detailed job descriptions. Use interviews and sample projects to evaluate candidates' abilities and fit. Building a reliable team of freelancers can help you scale your business while maintaining quality and efficiency.

Building a team involves hiring employees or contractors to handle various aspects of your business. This can include content creation, marketing, customer support, and more. Define clear roles and responsibilities, and provide training and support to ensure your team is aligned with your goals. Building a strong team allows you to scale your efforts and achieve greater success.

Expanding into new niches involves exploring additional areas of interest and opportunity. Research potential niches that complement your existing business and audience. Create content and promote affiliate products related to these new niches. Expanding into new niches diversifies your income streams and reduces risk.

Leveraging automation involves using tools and software to streamline repetitive tasks. Automation can include scheduling social media posts, sending email campaigns, and managing customer relationships. Use tools like Hootsuite, Mailchimp, and Zapier to automate your workflows. Automation saves time and increases efficiency, allowing you to focus on growth and strategy.

Case studies of scaling success can provide valuable insights and inspiration. Look at examples of affiliates who have successfully scaled their businesses and analyze their strategies. Pay attention to their growth tactics, outsourcing practices, and automation tools. Learning from their experiences can help you apply similar strategies to your own efforts.

Creating multiple streams of income involves diversifying your revenue sources. This can include promoting a variety of affiliate products, offering digital products, and providing services. Multiple income streams provide stability and reduce reliance on a single source of revenue. Diversification helps you build a more resilient and profitable business.

Investing in paid advertising can accelerate your growth and drive more traffic to your site. Use platforms like Google Ads, Facebook Ads, and Instagram Ads to reach a larger audience. Set clear goals and budgets for your campaigns, and continuously optimize them for better performance. Paid advertising can provide quick results and help you scale your efforts.

Scaling content production involves creating more high-quality content to attract and engage your audience. Use content calendars and planning tools to organize your content creation process. Collaborate with freelancers and team members to produce a variety of content formats, such as blog posts, videos, and infographics. Increasing your content output can drive more traffic and conversions.

Using advanced tools can enhance your scalability and performance. Invest in premium tools and software that provide advanced features and capabilities. This can include SEO tools, analytics platforms, and marketing automation software. Advanced tools help you optimize your efforts and achieve better results.

Improving workflow involves streamlining your processes to increase efficiency. Use project management tools like Trello, Asana, and Monday.com to organize tasks and collaborate with your team. Implement standard operating procedures (SOPs) for repetitive tasks to ensure consistency and quality. Efficient workflows save time and resources, allowing you to focus on growth.

Streamlining operations involves optimizing your business processes to reduce costs and increase productivity. This can include automating routine tasks, outsourcing non-core activities, and improving communication and collaboration. Streamlining operations helps you scale your business more effectively and achieve better results.

Building a brand involves creating a strong, recognizable identity for your business. Focus on developing a consistent brand message, visual identity, and tone of voice. Engage with your audience through content, social media, and customer interactions to build brand loyalty. A strong brand helps you stand out in a crowded market and attract more customers.

Case studies of brand building can provide valuable insights and inspiration. Look at examples of successful brands in your niche and analyze their strategies. Pay attention to their branding techniques, audience engagement, and marketing efforts. Learning from their success can help you build a stronger brand for your business.

Expanding your audience involves reaching new potential customers and growing your following. Use targeted marketing campaigns, social media strategies, and content collaborations to attract new visitors. Engage with your audience through email, social media, and other channels to build relationships and retain customers. Expanding your audience increases your reach and potential for conversions.

Creating high-ticket offers involves promoting products or services with higher price points and commissions. High-ticket items can significantly increase your earnings and provide more value to your customers. Research and select high-quality products that align with your audience's needs. Use persuasive content and targeted marketing to promote these offers.

Leveraging partnerships involves collaborating with other businesses and influencers to expand your reach. Partner with complementary brands and influencers to co-create content, run joint promotions, and cross-promote each other's products. Partnerships can help you reach new audiences and build credibility with potential customers.

International expansion involves reaching customers in different countries and regions. Research international markets and identify opportunities for growth. Create content and marketing campaigns tailored to specific regions and languages. Use international affiliate programs to promote products to a global audience. International expansion diversifies your market and increases your earning potential.

Maintaining quality is essential as you scale your business. Ensure that your content, products, and customer interactions consistently meet high standards. Regularly review and update your content to keep it relevant and valuable. Maintaining quality builds trust and loyalty with your audience and supports long-term growth.

Monitoring growth involves tracking your progress and making adjustments as needed. Use analytics tools to monitor key metrics, such as traffic, conversions, and earnings. Set regular checkpoints to review your performance and identify areas for improvement. Monitoring growth helps you stay on track and achieve your scaling goals.

Managing finances involves keeping track of your income and expenses, setting budgets, and planning for future growth. Use accounting software to organize your financial data and generate reports. Create a financial plan that includes savings, investments, and contingency funds. Effective financial management ensures your business remains profitable and sustainable.

Legal considerations involve understanding and complying with laws and regulations related to your business. This includes tax obligations, privacy policies, and affiliate disclosures. Consult with legal and financial professionals to ensure you're meeting all requirements. Staying compliant protects your business and reputation.

Planning for the future involves setting long-term goals and creating a roadmap for achieving them. Identify where you want your business to be in the next few years and outline the steps needed to get there. Regularly review and update your plan based on your progress and market changes. Future planning helps you stay focused and motivated.

As we move forward, it's time to focus on avoiding common pitfalls that can hinder your growth and success. By understanding and addressing these challenges, you can build a more resilient and successful affiliate marketing business.

Chapter 10: Avoiding Common Pitfalls

———

Avoiding common pitfalls is like navigating a maze; knowing where the traps are can help you find a clear path to success. In affiliate marketing, there are several common mistakes and challenges that can hinder your progress. By understanding these pitfalls and learning how to avoid them, you can build a more resilient and successful business.

Common affiliate marketing mistakes include neglecting content quality, ignoring audience needs, and failing to track performance. High-quality content is essential for attracting and retaining your audience. Neglecting content quality can lead to lower engagement and conversions. Always prioritize creating valuable and engaging content that addresses your audience's needs.

Staying compliant with laws and regulations is crucial for avoiding legal issues. This includes adhering to affiliate disclosure requirements, privacy policies, and advertising standards. Familiarize yourself with the laws and regulations in your region and ensure you're meeting all requirements. Staying compliant protects your business and reputation.

Avoiding black hat tactics is essential for maintaining trust and credibility. Black hat tactics include deceptive practices like keyword stuffing, cloaking, and spamming. These practices may provide short-term gains but can lead to penalties and long-term damage to your reputation. Focus on ethical marketing practices to build a sustainable business.

Handling rejection is a part of the affiliate marketing journey. Not every campaign will be successful, and not every product will resonate with your audience. Learn from your failures and use them as opportunities to improve. Stay resilient and keep experimenting with new strategies to find what works best for you.

Dealing with failure involves maintaining a positive mindset and staying motivated. Every failure is a learning opportunity that can help you grow and improve. Analyze what went wrong, make necessary adjustments, and move forward with a renewed focus. Persistence and resilience are key to overcoming challenges and achieving long-term success.

Managing time effectively is crucial for balancing your affiliate marketing efforts with other responsibilities. Create a schedule that allocates time for content creation, marketing, analysis, and personal activities. Use productivity tools and techniques, such as time blocking and task prioritization, to stay organized and efficient. Effective time management helps you maintain a healthy work-life balance.

Case studies of overcoming challenges can provide valuable insights and inspiration. Look at examples of affiliates who have faced and overcome obstacles in their journey. Analyze their strategies and learn from their experiences. Understanding how others have navigated challenges can help you avoid similar pitfalls and find solutions to your own problems.

Staying motivated involves setting clear goals, celebrating achievements, and maintaining a positive outlook. Affiliate marketing can be a challenging and sometimes solitary journey, so it's important to stay focused on your long-term vision. Surround yourself with supportive peers, take breaks when needed, and keep reminding yourself of your purpose and goals.

Avoiding burnout is essential for maintaining long-term productivity and motivation. Burnout can result from overworking, stress, and lack of balance. Prioritize self-care, take regular breaks, and set boundaries between work and personal life. Engage in activities that relax and rejuvenate you. Avoiding burnout helps you stay energized and focused on your goals.

Maintaining work-life balance involves setting clear boundaries and managing your time effectively. Allocate time for work, family, and personal activities, and stick to your schedule. Avoid overcommitting and learn to say no when necessary. A balanced approach ensures you remain productive and fulfilled in all areas of your life.

Handling negative feedback involves listening to your audience and making improvements based on their input. Negative feedback can provide valuable insights into areas where you can improve. Respond to criticism professionally and use it as an opportunity to grow. Addressing concerns and making necessary changes can strengthen your relationship with your audience.

Staying up-to-date with trends is essential for remaining competitive and relevant in the affiliate marketing industry. Follow industry news, subscribe to relevant blogs, and join online communities to stay informed about the latest developments. Continuously learning and adapting to changes in the market helps you stay ahead of the competition.

Networking with peers involves building relationships with other affiliates, marketers, and industry professionals. Join affiliate marketing forums, attend conferences, and participate in online communities. Networking provides opportunities for collaboration, learning, and support. Building a strong network can help you navigate challenges and achieve your goals.

Learning from mistakes involves analyzing what went wrong and making necessary adjustments. Mistakes are inevitable, but they can provide valuable learning opportunities. Reflect on your experiences, identify areas for improvement, and implement changes to avoid repeating the same mistakes. Learning from your mistakes helps you grow and improve your business.

Building resilience involves developing the ability to bounce back from setbacks and challenges. Resilience is essential for maintaining motivation and achieving long-term success. Cultivate a positive mindset, focus on your goals, and stay committed to your vision. Building resilience helps you navigate obstacles and stay on track.

Case studies of resilience in action can provide inspiration and practical tips. Look at examples of affiliates who have demonstrated resilience in the face of challenges. Analyze their strategies and learn from their experiences. Understanding how others have built resilience can help you develop your own strategies for overcoming obstacles.

Keeping ethical standards involves maintaining honesty, transparency, and integrity in your marketing practices. Disclose your affiliate relationships, provide accurate information, and prioritize the needs of your audience. Ethical marketing builds trust and credibility, which are essential for long-term success. Staying true to your values helps you build a sustainable business.

Managing expectations involves setting realistic goals and understanding that success takes time. Affiliate marketing is not a get-rich-quick scheme, and achieving your goals requires consistent effort and patience. Set achievable milestones, celebrate small wins, and stay focused on your long-term vision. Managing expectations helps you stay motivated and avoid disappointment.

Avoiding shiny object syndrome involves staying focused on your goals and avoiding distractions. Shiny object syndrome occurs when you're constantly tempted by new opportunities, tools, or strategies. While it's important to stay informed, constantly switching focus can hinder your progress. Prioritize your goals and stay committed to your plan.

Balancing multiple projects involves managing your time and resources effectively. If you're working on multiple affiliate marketing projects, create a schedule that allocates time for each one. Use project management tools to stay organized and track your progress. Balancing multiple projects requires careful planning and prioritization.

Knowing when to pivot involves recognizing when a strategy or project is not working and making necessary changes. Pivoting can involve changing your niche, content strategy, or marketing approach. Use data and insights to inform your decisions and be open to change. Knowing when to pivot helps you stay adaptable and resilient.

Long-term sustainability involves building a business that can adapt to changes and continue to grow. Focus on creating valuable content, building strong relationships with your audience, and staying informed about industry trends. Prioritize ethical practices and continuous improvement. Long-term sustainability ensures your business remains profitable and successful.

Continuous learning is essential for staying competitive and achieving long-term success. Stay curious, seek out new knowledge, and invest in your education. Attend workshops, read industry publications, and participate in online courses. Continuous learning helps you stay informed and improve your skills.

Seeking professional advice involves consulting with experts in areas where you need support. This can include legal, financial, and marketing professionals. Seeking advice ensures you're making informed decisions and staying compliant with laws and regulations. Professional guidance can help you avoid common pitfalls and achieve your goals.

As we wrap up, remember that success in affiliate marketing requires dedication, continuous learning, and a willingness to adapt. By avoiding common pitfalls and focusing on long-term growth, you can build a successful and sustainable affiliate marketing business. Embrace the journey, stay committed to your goals, and celebrate your achievements along the way.

www.ingramcontent.com/pod-product-compliance
Lightning Source LLC
Chambersburg PA
CBHW030036230526
45472CB00002B/532